ALL MY FRIENDS ARE ENGAGED

JEN GLANTZ

Thought Catalog Books
Brooklyn, NY

THOUGHT CATALOG BOOKS

Copyright © 2015 by Jen Glantz

All rights reserved.

Published by Thought Catalog Books, a division of The Thought & Expression Co., Williamsburg, Brooklyn. For general information and submissions: manuscripts@thoughtcatalog.com.

First edition, 2015.
ISBN 978-0692527153
10 9 8 7 6 5 4 3 2 1

Founded in 2010, Thought Catalog is a website and imprint dedicated to your ideas and stories. We publish fiction and non-fiction from emerging and established writers across all genres.

Cover photography by Wanqing Luo

To Lloyd, Laurie, Jason & Brandy Glantz:

Without you, I'd be a lost soul swimming in my very own fish bowl. I love you, with every mere morsel of my tap dancing heart, to the moon and back.

And, of course, to all the guys who were brave enough to take me on a first date:

Thank you. Sorry. I love you. Be well.

I remember the first date I ever went on. We were supposed to meet at the movies, but we ended up at different theaters. I told him it just wasn't meant to be and I went to watch the movie alone. The movie was 50 First Dates. – Jen Glantz

CONTENTS

1. There are (not) worse things than dating   7

2. Kiss, interrupted   11

3. Accidentally in love   14

4. My not so funny Valentine   19

5. Going once, going twice   24

6. Dating is awkward   29

7. 8 reasons he didn't ask for your phone number   33

8. All my friends are engaged   35

9. Mr. Wrong   40

10. 10 truths about dating no one will tell you   47

11. Online dating   51

12.	A week with a 100% honest online dating profile	57
13.	Love is blind	65
14.	9 unusual ways to describe what falling in love feels like	69
15.	Stop asking me why I'm single	72
16.	8 things I wish I told you on our date	76
17.	Why dating exit interviews should exist	79
18.	From auditioning for 'The Bachelor'	84
19.	How to deal with heartbreak	92
20.	The truth about being single on Valentine's Day	97
21.	Jewish "guilt" Filta fish	103
	Acknowledgements	109
	About the Author	111

CHAPTER 1.

THERE ARE (NOT) WORSE THINGS THAN DATING

Dating isn't the worst thing in the world.

She tells me over some moo goo gai pan at our favorite spot in the East Village. As if she has spent the last ten years of our lives on some other planet where first dates end in a swimmingly pleasant hug and an *I had a great time tonight* text message comes crawling right after the poor lad turns the corner.

My dates aren't like that, ever. They normally end with a painful head butt during an awkward goodbye and then, never hearing from the guy again—with the select few who reach out to tell me that the steak sauce or the red wine or the blonde roast coffee stain that I accidentally got on their button-down Ralph Lauren shirt has yet to come out.

But she's engaged, as are most of my friends these days. The girls in their mid-to-upper 20's with rocks the size of a full pimple living on their scrawny ring finger.

Well, excuse me, friends. Wasn't it just yesterday that we were pinky swearing away these cootie monsters during recess? Passing notes across Trigonometry class about how what's-his-face smells like apple juice or pee? Calling each other up after spoiled first dates to report how the guy spent 23 minutes spilling out tears over his ex-girlfriend and then slobbered all over your ear when he tried to turn in for a kiss?

What did I miss? Tell me!

Where was I after we walked off the stage at graduation and collectively had nothing and no one? I thought we were all in this together. Trying to navigate our early 20's and rummage together a resume to score a job that would pay enough dough for a moving truck and a one-way ticket to some bigger city, with dance floors that entertained our presence until 4am and apartments that made our dorm rooms seem like Bel Air mansions. Slowly making something beautiful out of the mess of our post-grad lives—*slow being the keyword here.*

How'd I get left behind, living at my parent's house in Boca Raton, Florida, spooning with Bop Bop, the giraffe stuffed animal, and an old Furbie with gum stuck in its hair? All while you were off whispering sweet nothings into the ear of Mr. Right.

It's as if one day I woke up, rubbed the mascara stains off my eyelids, and checked Facebook to find that all my friends were suddenly engaged.

Okay, so this isn't an advice book. If you thought its pages were scribbled with a ten-commandment sort of list that would make you a powerhouse dater, then you may want to stop reading now. Demand a full refund and use the money to buy yourself a box of munchkins from Dunkin Donuts or a Fudgie the Whale cake from Carvel—you'll surely need that more than this to help you navigate the dating world. And if you're looking for advice on things like how long you should wait before responding to his text message and what kinds of reach for your wallet tricks you should pull on a first date when the bill comes, well, you might want to toss this book in the recycling bin.

It's just a gigantic hug to everyone out there who is still single. The ones getting pestered regularly by their parents, their soon to be married friends, and their Rabbi, as to why they haven't found the "one" yet. And feeling the constant pressure, like the dry Arizona heat, to do something about it.

It's a book about the wildly hilarious mistakes we all make when we decide to stop acting human and start dating. Have you ever been on a date and wondered what the heck just came out of your mouth? You're jiggling with nervous shakes as you're trying to fill a gap of silence, talking about how much you absolutely love to go deep sea diving, but really the ocean gives you the heebie jeebies.

Let's just get one thing straight: dating is awkward. Anyone who tells you differently is either blinded by the twinkle of their engagement ring or having a temporary lapse in memory over the time in their lives when they were once wedged into playing a one-sided game of 20 questions with a guy who has broccoli stuck in his teeth.

So, if you're ready to continue, we can start this off in the same fashion most of my first dates begin:

Hi, I'm Jen. It's very nice to meet you and I'm really sorry about what you're about to experience.

CHAPTER 2.

KISS, INTERRUPTED

At 5-years-old, I was certain that I knew everything about:

1. The ins and outs of being the pink Power Ranger during recess.
2. How to decipher which multi-colored mat would give me the best ZZZ's during naptime.
3. That McDonalds french fries were way better than the soggy ones that Burger King sold.
4. Oh, and love.

The depths of our hearts were as thick as a piece of red construction paper and our futures were limited to the make-believe skits we'd dream up in our play kitchens. But there I was, at age 5, wearing a pair of bubble-gum pink corduroy Osh

Kosh B'gosh overalls, with virgin blonde hair that was stained with hints of chlorine and chocolate milk, falling madly in love. All while the other little girls shrilled that boys had cooties and were seemingly creepier looking than the monsters that were hanging out underneath their twin-size princess beds.

Scott had shaggy brown hair and I knew I loved him the very second that we met, when we were promoted to be co-line leaders. He was the generous I'll trade you my string cheese for your gummy bears kind of boy and one afternoon, as we sat underneath the homemade rocket ship that was resting in the center of our kindergarten classroom, he kissed me on the cheek.

In that exact moment, I imagined that I had this great big world of recess and Disney movies all figured out.

See, we'd finish up kindergarten before living happily ever after, with our blow up swim floaties and car seats. Barbie and Teresa would be my loyal bridesmaids and I'd grow up to be a stuffed animal collector, and Scott, well he'd be a firefighter or an astronaut. Up to him.

His fruit-punch dyed lips stained the side of my face and just as I went to kiss him back, to let him know that our love was more real than the tooth fairy, I watched Scott turn away from me and kiss another girl. The same floozy who had invited me over for a play date and spit cookie on my hair when we were climbing the monkey bars. I watched him kiss her soft, plump cheeks in the same delicate fashion that he smooched mine.

And so at 5, I was certain that I learned everything I ever needed to know about love:

1. Never trust a boy wearing jorts.
2. And, that love was as messy as finger painting. Sometimes you'd mix two colors together and be left with an overwhelmingly beautiful display that you'd eagerly bring home to your mother. And sometimes, more often than you would like, you're left with a gobbledygook combination that you'd have to throw out. You would just have to start over. To scrub your hands clean, drink a Capri Sun, eat a couple of graham crackers and try again.

CHAPTER 3.

ACCIDENTALLY IN LOVE

I was an English major in college with a strong affinity for math, and much of that I owed to a boy named Paul.

At the University of Central Florida, where the total amount of students equals the entire population of Wyoming, all freshmen are forced to take a basic math class called College Algebra. It doesn't matter if you are majoring in marine biology, or philosophy, or as my good pal Samantha was, *undeclared* with a minor in *I'll figure it out next year.*

On day one of College Algebra, I took a seat in the first row of a movie theater style classroom that was overflowing with 450 18-year-olds who just freed themselves from their parent's house and bought a 4-year pass into this amusement park called college. I ended up in the first row partially because my vision was a disgrace and I refused to wear my glasses and partially because

I arrived about 10 minutes late and that was the very last seat available.

Sitting on my immediate left was a silky brown haired boy with a wrinkly AC/DC t-shirt and a backpack that looked like it had been places. Not places like the supermarket or the beach or a field trip to Sea World, but places. Foreign countries that I've only flirted with on maps and backstage at rock concerts of bands that made love to songs I listened to on repeat.

We're in the middle of learning about quadratic equations when he turns to me and says, *Paul*, before finishing off his greeting with a flimsy handshake.

I feel my cheeks begin to shock with the color red and before I've finished plotting my most delicate response, our fingers meet and I say, *I'm Jen, yep that's me!* Loud enough that the echo of my short monologue drifted all the way to the back of the room. Loud enough, that the professor paused her lecture to stare and let me know, on day one, that she would never forget my name.

As I got to know Paul, I got to know someone on this planet who was worse at math than I was. We'd be trying to solve for X and he'd spend fifteen minutes arguing over the unparalleled decision of some academic slob who chose these unpopular letters for math equations. But the day Paul, the finance major, asked me to tutor him, was the day I spent about three hours tutoring myself, first.

The afternoon after we took our first math exam, Paul asked to walk me diagonally across the campus to my Spanish class. We hit the front door of the building right before he proposed the idea of hanging out with me on Friday night. Not tutor him. Not listen to one of his rants about some philosophical mongrel, but hang out. I replied with a smile and as we separated, as Paul went to turn left and I went to turn right, so that I could learn how to say something I'd never need to know how to say in Spanish, I said to him:

Bye Paul, I love you.

His head jolted and his eyeballs began doing backflips. His feet were salsa dancing in circles, trying to decide whether to exit the building or just stand still.

I closed my eyes as tightly as possible, hoping deep down to the peanut butter and jelly resting in my stomach that I didn't just say those words out loud. But I did. I said them in the same overly casual and meaningless way we quickly tell our friends goodbye, love you, after spending the afternoon getting brunch or flipping through the clearance racks at Bloomingdales with them.

Had I loved him? No. Absolutely not. I was 18 and I had no idea what that word meant or why people took it so seriously. Love was a term I reserved for my family and really fluffy pets that I shot goo-goo eyes at when I visited the dog store. Paul and I and love fit together like a flawed logarithm in algebra class. There were errors and mistakes and I didn't mean to say it. I didn't mean to say anything.

But I did. Loud enough that the few people trickling into their classes also heard and watched in painful disbelief. I had witnesses.

When Paul gained his sense of direction and his paws were able to push open the exit door, he left. I never heard from him again. He stopped coming to math class.

He must have thought I meant it. He must have thought that after I said it, I wanted a diamond ring, a house with a yard and a golden retriever. He must have thought that math had a way over people and I in particular had this crazy way over him.

And then two years later, at a meeting for Habitat for Humanity, I was in line to sign up to do a service project painting the walls of a house in downtown Orlando when I looked across the room and there he was.

And there I was, salsa dancing in place over whether or not I should say hello or exit the building. But before my mind could deliberate on a decision, I watched him watch me and give me an open palm tree kind of wave in the distance before grabbing the hand of a girl and tugging her out the door.

It would be many years until I ever said those words to someone again. And when I did, it would be formulated and thought about and said to a person who I believed showed me what love was. It would be said slowly, as my voice cracked and my wrists trembled, and it would be meant to last forever. Though sometimes it doesn't. Sometimes even when we wait very long to tell a person we love them, they too will walk away one day.

Maybe love is something we're meant to say casually and not regard as a prize from a treasure chest that a person earns. Perhaps even if we don't take love seriously or perhaps if we do, we'll end up with exactly the same thing. Nothing.
Or everything. It just depends, but it doesn't depend on timing.

I bumped into Paul minutes after he threw me a *you're somebody that I used to know* wave, but now his hands and his mouth were fully occupied. As I tried to slip by him, I could hear the faint surrender of the words he was tossing into the ears of a girl he seemed totally overwhelmed by. As if his prime numbered self finally found some kind of match. And as I walked right past them, his whisper into her ear traveled a few feet away and collapsed right into mine.

Goodbye, he said so flawlessly and blasé, *I love you.*

CHAPTER 4.

MY NOT SO FUNNY VALENTINE

I had my first real Valentine at the age of 20.

Before that, I spent the 14th of February as the team captain in charge of rounding up troops of my single friends to balance out the weight on my couch, as we stuffed handfuls of sprinkled cupcakes into our mouths. Scoops of vanilla icing and greeting cards from my parents were my idea of a Valentine's Day gone right.

This was all until I got a phone call the night before that dreaded day from a guy I'd been on a first date with a week earlier. He wanted to take me out for Valentine's Day.

Are you sure? I protested. Kind of shying away from the idea of spending it with an actual person who wasn't comatose from an elevated level of sugar intake.

Our first date was as memorable as a lecture in my Theory of Literature class, as he struggled to answer most of my questions in complete sentences and the only things I realized we had in common was our hometown and April birthdays. He had a love affair with pulled pork and I was a lifetime vegetarian. But a date on Valentine's Day was something that my troop of single gal pals would never want me to refuse.

That year, for the first time, my spot on the couch would be auctioned off to some other lonely girl.

When I exited my apartment at 7pm sharp, I was focused on balancing my nervous body that was planted inside of heels two-sizes-too-big from my roommate's closet, since my collection of shoes only included a dense variety of converse. And so, I wobbled toward his car that I noticed was parked on the side of the road.

It was only after I opened the car door, sat down in the passenger seat, buckled my seat belt and turned to the left, that I realized the guy I was cozying up next to, reaching over for a bear hug, was not my date.

I was in the wrong car.

Ten seconds of listening to a screaming guy, wrapped up in a tuxedo with slicked back hair, was enough to release me from a paralyzed state of shock, and pull my flustered self together to open the car door and leave.

My cheeks were scorching hot as I entered the correct car and though I tried to write off the situation that he was just a front-row witness to, he didn't find it funny. He shook his head in disbelief, as if I had just pantsed him in public or entered his car doing giant kicks to the side like I was the star of some Gloria Estefan conga line.

So, now that I'm here and you're here, where are we off to? I asked. Curiously trying to change the subject.

I hope you're excited, he said. And I was, it was definitely the runner up emotion to feeling embarrassed. *Because we're going to a steakhouse.*

Oh, that sounds great. I said, figuring he must have just forgotten that I'm a vegetarian. I told myself I wouldn't make a big deal out of it. I'd stuff my face with salad and French fries and try to have a good time.

We arrived and he handed me a plastic, single, rose before he reached into his pocket for something I hoped was a chocolate Hershey kiss, but a perpetually single girl can only dream.

I know you're a vegetarian, he said as he fingered a tiny envelope that was hanging out of his pocket, *but my Uncle gave me a gift certificate to this steakhouse and I had no one else to go with. So I figured it would work for Valentine's Day, with you.*

At 20, we're still figuring out how to date and even more so, how to make it through an entire date without throwing our hands in the air and surrendering. Plus, we were 30 minutes away from campus and my cellphone had given up on me and died. My only option was to just sit there.

And I did. I sat there as the waiter brought over different slabs of meat and asked my date to choose his feast. I sat there as we split a dessert and before I could get my spoon in the chocolate lava cake, he finished the whole thing. And, I sat there and smiled when the waiter came around with a camera and snapped a photo of us, a phony couple together on this memorable evening.

When the date ended, his tires rolled over the very same spot outside of my apartment where I mistakenly got into the wrong car, with the wrong guy, who was probably doing the right things to make his date feel special, tonight.

Well, happy Valentine's Day, I said before I didn't say anything else to him, ever.

You too, he whispered as the car door clicked shut.

I took the elevator up to the 4th floor and fished around my purse for the keys to get inside. The keys to a place I knew just a few hours ago was filled with a group of single girls dressed up in wacky neon pink outfits, belting out the lyrics to Spice Girls songs and cheering on their mutual best friend Carrie Bradshaw through the other end of the TV set. Tomorrow they'd come rushing into my room and demand answers. Wanting to know the scent of his cologne, the sound of his laugh, and the feel of his raw lips. They'd want to know what it felt like to have had the one thing they didn't that night, *somebody*.

And I didn't want to disappoint them. I didn't want them to think I was hopeless, that we were all hopeless, in trying to find the person who would keep our hearts spinning like the tip of a dreidel.

I'll figure out something to tell them, tomorrow, I told myself. *But until then, I just want to sit here, alone.*

I flipped on the TV and shoved a handful of heart candies into my mouth before dropping one on the floor. I picked it up and gave it a glance to read the words on it before eagerly digesting it.

You & Me, it read.

And I couldn't help but laugh.

CHAPTER 5.

GOING ONCE, GOING TWICE

He starts the bidding at $10 before he reads off a handwritten index card.

Up next we have Jen Glantz.

I climb up a short flight of stairs and strut on over to the X in the middle of the stage.

Jen likes to play guitar.

And I bust out some air guitar. My teased blonde hair and black lined eyes make me look a little bit like C.C. Deville from Poison.

And well, look at that, she once ate pizza for 15 days in a row.

And I act like I'm in a pizza-eating contest, showing off how I can devour a slice in less than 2 minutes.

Jen will rock your world.

I finish the game of charades by throwing up a peace sign to a crowd of people who are uncomfortably silent. Visibly choking back their urge to vomit up laughter in my face.

***

I'm drenching a cucumber sushi roll in an overflowing dish of soy sauce, about to shove it into my mouth, with my friend Seth, when all of a sudden, the doors to the restaurant fling open and there she is.

You're never going to believe this.

And before I can even begin throwing out 20 questions of how she found me, why she's here, and what she's about to tell me that I won't believe, my roommate is flailing her arms with excitement, acting like she's come here to tell me something overwhelmingly grand. As if she's about to say our joint purchased lottery ticket just won us $347 million, or that we both, somehow, passed astronomy class.

Beweave what? I struggle to get out while I'm chomping down on a roll the size of my earlobe.

The school's having a date auction to raise money for a charity tonight and I, your #1 friend, got you a spot. You're going to be auctioned off.

I'm silent.

Hello! Earth to Jen! Do you understand what's about to happen?

I go back to munching on my sushi, pretending that her and her news are merely just a post-astronomy exam hallucination.

Some gorgeous guy is going to pay money to take you out on a date.

She grabs me by the arm. Throws out my half-eaten Bento Box and drags me to the car.

You only have 45 minutes before you're on. Shower, shave, and Jen, she says as if I need the friendly reminder, *wear something that's not wrinkled. Something that matches.*

Being the single friend in the group often elicits unnecessary babysitters. The friends who are constantly checking up on you, as if being single means you absolutely are unable to be a functioning member of society. They'll drop by with their constant *are you okay* text messages, followed up by their *how are you spending your Saturday night, do you want to spend it with John and I* phone calls. And even if most of my Saturday nights revolve around watching old episodes of *Gossip Girl* and getting Insomnia cookies delivered, it doesn't mean I *need* watchdogs.

But, I hadn't been on a date all semester. Plus, really, how bad could it be? If I just stand up there with my shoulders back and flash a Miss America smile every now and then, guys will be bidding their financial aid reimbursement money on me in no time. Right?

***

I'm officially drenched in sweat when I finish my game of charades and the emcee is done trying to sell me like a piece of art at an auction.

But, most people are crossing their arms, squishing their eyebrows and trying to figure out if I am indeed the most awkward person they have ever come across.

And maybe I am, at least in this moment. I'm starting to get desperate and I'm grilling my friend Seth, trying to mouth to him:

Get...me...out...of...here.

But he's laughing, and like most of the crowd he's not making any sudden moves.

How about $15...anyone?

The crowd is silent.

There's one guy in the way back who puts his arm half up in the sky. Could it be? And if so, what a great story we will one day tell our kids about how we met.

But his brisk arm motion is not body language for *I'd like to place a bid*, it's just him signaling his friend across the room to get the heck out of there.

I wanted out too. I tried to run off the stage but the emcee grabs me and whispers inside of a smile:

Hey, you're not going anywhere, just relax.

It was my good friend Seth who made the final and only bid. He waved a 20-dollar bill in the air and told the emcee to keep the change if they just let me off the stage.

I fell into Seth's arm, overwhelmed with embarrassment and covered in my own stress sweat. But before I could cry, before I could digest any of what just happened or what didn't happen, he rubs down the hair that's sticking up on my head and says to me as if none of this ever occurred:

Let's go finish our sushi.

CHAPTER 6.

DATING IS AWKWARD

A List of Awkward Things That Have Happened To Me On Dates:
How I dealt with them vs. how I should have dealt with them

1. We're at a Mexican restaurant and my date pauses from stuffing a burrito in his mouth because he feels something thick oozing from his nostril holes.

Is my nose bleeding? He asks.

It's not bleeding, it's gushing. It's splatter painting the mushy rice that's getting all cozy with the beans and the guacamole of his meat-in-a-blanket burrito.

How I handled it: *No, I don't think so?* I said, because I didn't know what else to do. This is what I get for being smack in the middle of a debate over whether or not ObamaCare is really, actually, a good thing. If rule #346 in the dating manual is don't bring up politics on a first date, rule #347 should be when your date asks if there's a Niagara Falls of blood spilling out of their nose, don't lie.

When I should have: Offered him a jumbo tampon from my purse and stuck it in his nose to clog the mess that was beginning to stain the crisp white tablecloths at this fine dining establishment.

2. The restaurant is cash only. He has a five-dollar bill and I have about $1.37 in spare change that has gum attached to it from living on the bottom of my purse.

How I handled it: Mushed together his and mine, threw in a Bed Bath Beyond coupon and bribed the waitress that if she let us off from paying the reminder $35.62 that she'd have unlimited karma points, and in a city that works off that voodoo it could really come in handy. Especially when you're trying to catch the 6 train or walking to work in the morning trying to avoid a cab splashing water on your white work pants.

When I should have: Stayed quiet. Kept the coupon my mom mailed me for 20% off a new vacuum and offered to hit up an ATM for my share of the spaghetti that I devoured during our little Lady and the Tramp shindig.

3. Our date is coming to an end, and right as I go to put my second lanky hand through the arm

of my jacket, I knock over a row of (full, half full, none of them were empty) wine glasses.

How I handled it: Said I'm sorry over and over and over again that it sounded like I was making a dubstep track and then, I bent down and started collecting the pieces of sticky broken glass. All while my date started to tip toe out the door, pretending he didn't know me.

When I should have: Screamed Opa! or L'Chaim!

4. I've got my meat hooks around a really good looking guy, as we're watching the sun fall asleep on Sunset Avenue, when my shoe gets stuck in the crack of a sidewalk and splits open.

How I handled it: There I was, face down smooching the uneven pavement, trying not to call attention to the giant gash that was making my kneecap spurt out blood. Trying not to call attention to my left foot, which was now naked and exposed, peeping out of my split open GUESS shoe.

When I should have: This was just a lose-lose situation that would ultimately leave me barefoot and alone.

5. We're at Salad Creations and my date is on his phone the entire time. But not to check his Facebook or text his mother or play a round of

Candy Crush, he's in the middle of a 35-minute conversation with someone else.

How I handled it: Swirled the remaining vegetables in my bowl together to form funny faces until it was time to leave.

When I should have: Pulled out my phone and called him. Assuming he'd accept my call, I would have then asked him if he'd like to hang up with whoever was on the other line and actually be on a date with, hmmm, I don't know, me?

6. In the middle of drinks at a Speakeasy in the Lower East Side, my date turns to me and says, Wow, Jen, you're way smarter than you look.

How I handled it: ::silence::

When I should have: I'm still trying to figure this one out. Really.

CHAPTER 7.

8 REASONS HE DIDN'T ASK FOR YOUR PHONE NUMBER

1. He's stuck in 1999 and only has a beeper and beepers don't store phone numbers. I'll start with this one because it's really, truly, the most unlikely reason—yet, when you are running through different potential play-by-plays as to why someone didn't ask for your number (or call you, or ask you on a date, etc.), you'll always, without a doubt, start with the most absurd possibility first.

2. In serendipity, he trusts. The good ol' if it's meant to be, then we will of course run into each other again at some undisclosed location, in one of the five boroughs, before winter kicks our butts back into hibernation.

3. Maybe he's not fully convinced you're into him. Your "resting" face can be misleading and though your heart is pumping gimme gimme more, you're face is all like I've had one too many glasses of merlot and even though my bright eyes are closing, I'm all here with you, babe.

4. He's too nervous. It can be that simple, really.

5. He has a girlfriend and/or a boyfriend. Mazel Tov to them.

6. He's just not interested in ever seeing you again. This one's a bit ugly to digest.

7. Three is such an overwhelming and defunct crowd. You, him, your sorority sisters. And while this poor lad is struggling to spark your interest with amassing conversation, he also has to give some love to your gal pal and her nucleolus of dirty looks that shoot threats as bold as *don't you dare break her heart or I'll tell my 5,489 Twitter followers what a baboon you are.*

8. You didn't give him yours. Oh wait, you didn't know this was an option did you? There's no footnote in your self-help dating bible that reads, "If you like a guy YOU should do something about it?" Give him your digits, your AIM screen name, your e-mail address. Whatever you're comfortable with. If he contacts you, he contacts you.

CHAPTER 8.

ALL MY FRIENDS ARE ENGAGED

Gosh, my palms are getting sweaty just thinking about this. Maybe that's the reason I'm not engaged, I sweat too much or I talk about sweating too much or I fear that when I go on a date and the poor lad goes in for a hug hello, I'll soak through his fine pressed button-down shirt with a puddle of *I hope there's not lipstick on my teeth* sweat that accumulated on my dash over here from the F train.

I whimsically believed, I really did, that when I graduated from college I knew exactly the ins and outs of how life was going to smack me in the face. I thought I could grasp the semi-precious reality of moving back in with my parents after living underneath a pile of my own stench in a never-cleaned, do-what-I-want, dorm room for four years. Or the vulgar process of trying to get a job, a real job, where people wear suits and demand 3 sugars in their espresso, that would pay enough bucks to afford my basic needs: electricity, Jell-O, toilet paper–for crying out loud!

But never, not once, in my four years of pre-requisite classes did anyone sit me down and give me the birds and the bees kind of lecture that just a few minutes after my mommy framed my diploma, all my compadres would jump ship and get engaged.

That while I was off, lugging around a beat up brief case of strangled career dreams, hitchhiking across state lines, and getting my mug shot taken for overdue library fines, they'd be off doing the Argentine Tango with the person they dared to spend the rest of their lives with. The one that would still have the gory guts to make eye contact with them through morning breath, afternoon milk mustaches, and evening burps.

People who never even went on a date in college are suddenly stomping on glass, smooching L'Chaims, and saying, "I do."

Really?

In college, I hazily remember the only thing most of you would ever remotely commit to saying *I do* to was Jager bomb, after Jager Bomb, after, ah what's the point, I'll save the rest for your Bachelorette party toast.

I'm only jealous of your life, your conjugal state of mind, 76% of the time. Frankly, the only time it gives me the heebie jeebies is when Facebook decides to flash food your new engagement all over my newsfeed, but I've learned to deal with my feelings, mostly through interpretive dancing.

I'd most like it if people just stopped talking about me being single like they talk about damaged goods, or animals that are about to get neutered or something silly like gingivitis. After I'm done kvetching over my latest mind-boggling date where a guy made me shell out $50 for his meal, and mine, instead of putting your draped with diamonds finger over the small of my back and saying something brilliantly pathetic like *There will be more fish in that cesspool of a sea*, offer to go to town with me on a pie of pizza or halfsies on a black and white cookie. That's all I really need, someone to consume half of my *in the name of misery* calories.

So listen up, all you engaged folk:

I don't want to be set up with the boy who sits across from you in your work cubicle that you watch picking his nose or the one who is *in the process* of breaking up with his long-term, long-distance, long-standing pain in the neck girlfriend of 8 years. I'm going to say a definite NO WAY to the one who *Isn't your type* and you wouldn't date, but maybe, just oh maybe, I'd like him. I'll pass.

Don't tell me it's time to maybe explore setting up an online profile, unless you're talking about one on Myspace and if so, then I already have those Internet waves covered, thank you.

And don't treat me like I'm a hurricane victim. I'm okay. I don't need to come over for a home cooked meal, or to watch *X Factor* or for a slumber party where we can braid each other's hair and read *Teen Vogue*. I do my thing, my own thing. I get Chinese food delivered on the regular, go out to bars in the Village and get grouped by "bros" smelling like Jose Cuervo in their cut off t's. (Stop me when you're too jealous of my single life, please.)

I'm single, but there's nothing wrong with me. [Okay, well maybe a couple of things. Like I eat with my hands, cover up awkward silences by talking in hamster-spinning circles, engage in political debates on the first date, and wear knee socks, in the summer]. But that's it, I've told you all my flaws. Now I hope we can proceed with that calm feeling you possess after you rip a Band-Aid off the hairiest part of your arm.

They say you meet people where you spend the most time and in that case, I think I'll be fine. I spend 1/3 of my time on Twitter, 1/3 in my bed and the other 1/3 is distributed between gym, tan, and laundry.

Engage in my happiness for you, and spare me the pity, okay?

I'm very happy for all the people I know, or Facebook reminds me I know, who are getting married. It's such an exquisite gem to meet your soul mate in this world. The person who will forever spend the rest of your days with you as your heart rises and falls likes your expanding waistline and you start to get the three c's: cavities, cellulite and crust (and I'm not talking about pizza crust). As a single girl living in NYC, having guys spill drinks on my toes at bars or turn out to be circus freaks 5 minutes into a date, if you find a person who makes your heart beat like an Avicii song and who can whisk you away like the Chicago winds, I'm happy for you, I really am, from the bottom of my triathlon-running heart.

I just hope, I really do, that all of you will remember me, and hopefully will still be physically able to do the Electric Slide with me, at my wedding, someday.

CHAPTER 9.

MR. WRONG

I'm always entertained by the thought that I'll meet the love of my entire life in a bookstore. As I'm fingering through chapter two of *Catcher in the Rye*, melting over the part where Holden goes to visit his teacher Mr. Spencer, I'd look up and there he'd be. Maybe he's flipping through another Salinger classic like *Franny and Zooey* or *Nine Stories*, but when he sees me, he stops. Instead of asking to buy me a drink or spitting out some kind of rehearsed pickup line, he'll simply say something geeky and adorable like, *Did you ever wonder if the real reason Salinger was such a recluse was because he had really bad halitosis?*

And we'll laugh before he asks me out for coffee, before we spend the rest of our lives together.

But it doesn't work like that.

We don't get to decide where we'll meet the person we fall in love with or the ones we'll spend all winter with licking the hot chocolate mustaches off their face. And as our generatiᵒ turns their heads down and focuses on blabbering to each other through text messages or Twitter or on the anonymous comments section of websites, while sitting in the confines of their own apartments, binging on Netflix and ordering in take-out so they don't have to put on pants, the prospect of meeting someone offline, has become, perhaps, extinct.

Meeting at a networking event has become, *we connected with each other on LinkedIn.*

What used to be bumping into someone while playing air guitar at a Guns N' Roses concert, has become *I fell in love with him after I followed his playlist on Spotify.*

And when someone says they *met through mutual friends*, it's likely they are talking about how one of them came across the other posting a picture of their old college pal.

The thrill of a blind date is now spoiled thanks to the power of an invasive Google search, and you have the option to find 6 ways to Sunday worth of photos of someone's face by a quick scroll through their Instagram.

But in this story, I met him out at a bar. Which usually, always, is the driving force behind my motivation to leave the bag of caramel drizzled popcorn and fuzzy pajama shorts behind to go out with a group of friends on a Saturday night.

Who knows who I'll meet? I tell myself as I'm sorting through a mental pro-con list over whether or not I should leave the confines of my pillow top mattress. *And if I stay in my apartment, well, the only people I'll meet are the delivery guys who drop off my cheese quesadillas and the man in the building across the street who likes to clip his toenails out the window.*

I'm out in the West Village when a guy nervously approaches me, not with a pickup line or a handshake, but with a magic trick. One that starts with his subway card in his hand, shredded into three pieces, and ends with it perfectly put together underneath my stool. We're spitting out conversation about the song that's playing, and the best pizza spot in the city, and how my friends that are circling him with threatening looks shouldn't alarm him. I make mention that I'm a huge Mets fan before he asks me out to go see them play at their next home game.

So, the very next Saturday, I meet him at the ballpark. He tells me he's standing underneath the Citi Field sign, wearing blue shorts and a white-striped shirt. And though a heavy crowd of fans weave around me in an eager haste to get inside and soak their hot dogs in a nice cold beer, I find him almost immediately.

I'm walking toward him and his face is relaxed, so I walk even more toward him and start waving fervently, as if I'm a teenager trying to catch the attention of a member of One Direction. But still, even then, nothing. He's acting like he's never seen me before, like I must be waving to the mother and her three small children that are standing inches behind him.

But as I reach him, and I stop right in front of him, his eyes seem to bulge and his mouth seems to swoosh and slowly, as he's trying to put it together that I'm the girl he's invited to this game, I'm starting to realize he must have been so brutally wasted the night we met that he has no idea who I am. It's seconds before he stops looking at me like I'm some kind of monster of a stranger, a person he's never met in his life before, or an alien. One of the two. And even until this day, I'm not entirely sure which.

Hello? I say, as I'm finally as close to him as two people can be without making a motion to touch each other.

Oh...um..hi? He says, before I force him into a hug. *That's what you're wearing?*

He's flustered over the fact that I'm a) not the dream girl his drunken mind concocted from the other night, and b) I'm clothed in a Mets shirt that's 5 sizes too big for my figure and jean shorts. As if he expected me to arrive in a tight mini skirt and a tube top.

We're at a baseball game, I remind him, but somehow my choice of attire is just absolutely ludicrous.

43

We take our seats right behind home plate and I'm fishing to make conversation carry on with a person who likes me just as much as he likes baseball.

Most people are turned off from the game for the same reasons that I love it: it's slow paced, stop-and-go kind of feel can make it drag on forever, and I'm absolutely dazzled by that excitement. But suddenly, on this Saturday, those people are right. Four and a half hours of foul balls and players walking to first base, and 105 degree heat that's making my body perspire so much that it looks like I just peed in my freaking pants. And if he asks, I'll say I did. Because maybe if he thinks I peed in my pants, he'll leave. And then I can spend the rest of the afternoon with a team of guys who like baseball better than they can play—but at least they like something! Instead, we're just two strangers who are both just overwhelmingly pissed off about this current situation for two very different reasons.

Him, because I look less like Heidi Klum and more like Ke$ha. And me, well, because I wanted to eat pizza and the ballpark ran out of it.

When it ended, when both teams shook hands and walked off the field, so did we. And as I'm riding the F train back into the city, I'm sulking in my very damp clothing and first-date misery, alone.

There's a mother and her son across from me on the train and they're talking about how lost they've been getting wandering around the city all day. And the son tells her, *it seems like I'm always turning the wrong direction.*

And boy do I feel him.

That's alright, she says, *because you can only turn the wrong direction once before you realize the right way to go, and then, then you just keep going.*

And I wondered if that applied to love, too. All of us have a rolodex of horrible dating stories. About guys who act like both Jekyll and Hyde, or are still madly in love with their ex-girlfriends, or who get so plastered on a first date that they end up passed out in their bowl of clam chowder. And even my closest friends, the ones who are now twirling their hearts around the love of their lives, have also suffered through pathetically torturous dates before. I've sat next to them just as many times as they've sat next to me, patting each other's backs and going halves on a pint of banana pudding, listening to one another sob that we'll never meet the one, that after this date or that one, we feel so hopelessly lost. That we'll never find the right time, the right way, the right person to love.

Right, the boy tells his mom before they both rush off the subway car, fearless about getting so completely lost in this complicated and tremendously gorgeous city.

And as I scurry up the stained subway stairs, the same ones so many people have climbed up before me, I find myself back on 33rd and Park, back at my beginning, my starting point, my home plate.

CHAPTER 10.

10 TRUTHS ABOUT DATING NO ONE WILL TELL YOU

I've read three dating advice books in my entire life:

He's Just Not That Into You — which after I read it, made me think no guy I dated was actually, 100%, into me.

Why Men Love Bitches — which also made me feel as though any guy I dated after was not really into me.

And, Patti Stanger's book, which the only advice I actually remember from it had to do with her saying that guys don't want to date girls who air their relationship stories out to the world. It looks like I'm doomed. *Thanks, Patti.*

So, do me a favor. Will you? Take your stack of worn-out, tear-stained, dating advice books and throw them out. Toss them in the recycling bin, use them as coasters on your living room table, glue them on top of each other and make them into a sturdy step stool. Just don't read them anymore, okay?

All they'll do is twist your thoughts, your judgments and your actions around like a tangled computer chord, leaving you acting like some kind of robotic monster who says and does things completely out of character.

Remember, only, these tips:

1. If you want to meet new people (potential dates) you need to actually try. Stop letting your couch cushions and your Netflix account and your Saturday girl's nights (where you ONLY dance and talk to each other) keep on inhibiting you from meeting people. Go to a meet-up event. Start shaking hands with strangers. Set up an online account on a website you're open to giving a try. Just start by stopping to look down at your phone all the time while you're out in public and say Hello more.

2. If it's not passionate, I-can't-stop-thinking-about-you kind of love, what's the point? Too many things in life are just mundane and blasé, love shouldn't be. The person who latches onto your heart should make you feel extraordinary. There's absolutely no point in settling down just to settle.

3. Write down a list of things you love in this world and a list of things that bother you. Start to understand who you are a bit more and then, after it's spelled out on paper, begin to love yourself in such an unconditional way. Own up to the quirks and habits and hobbies that make you, you. That way, when someone enters your life, you'll be able to dazzle them with confidence.

4. Find an example. Your parents. Friends of yours. The 96-year-old couple in matching burgundy sweaters splitting French toast at the diner across the street, looking at each other like they just met for the first time. Find comfort in knowing that that crazy little thing called love does, in fact, exist.

5. If it doesn't feel right, it's not. Don't ignore the red flags that wave frantically at you, like a teenager trying to catch the attention of a member of One Direction, on dates 1-3.

6. Never say you're too busy for love. Because you're not. It's an excuse. It's one of those things we tell ourselves because we desperately want to believe it. If you want something bad enough, you'll somehow find the time to do it, to have it, to hold onto it.

7. Treat love like you do books. When it gets boring, or too complicated, put it down. Skip to the end.

8. If by date #4, you're questioning your interest in a person, call it quits. Don't waste time letting something drag on that's not meant to be—likewise, don't force something that's not meant to be.

9. Don't hold back. Talk about whatever you want. Order your favorite dish of chicken parm and eat it on a first date. If you put on a costume and adopt someone else's personality, you're just delaying the inevitable: the person getting to know the real you. If you're not sure who the real you is, that's okay, please refer back to #3.

10. Do only what feels right. If you want to text the person after the date to say thank you for the nice night out, or after the third date give them a smooch goodbye, do it. The worst part of doing a case study on shredded love is having your memories corrupted by all the things you wish you did.

CHAPTER 11.

ONLINE DATING

I distinctly remember when I was a little girl, consumed with playing with pretty little Barbie dolls in neon pleather outfits and had a thirst for digging for worms in moist soil, my elders surrounding me, fingering the tips of my chlorine infested hair and telling me these exact instructions:

When you grow up, Jennifer, they said as they pinched my cheeks ever so tightly that it looked like I put on a little too much Estee Lauder blush, *the boys will be knocking down your door.*

Well, here I am. I'm 25, soon to be 26, living in NYC, in an apartment with four sturdy walls and what do you know—a door! A door with a doorbell, for crying out loud, so if a nice charmer wanted to come over and had too many gifts to shower me with in his hands, he wouldn't have to fumble around trying to knock, he could just ring the freaking doorbell.

It's silent around here.

The only people who come knocking are delivery men, who know me, intimately, by the side dishes I order with my dumplings, and my non-gregarious neighbors who knock frantically to tell me to stop pretending I'm Jimmy Page by rocking out on the guitar at the measly hour of 2 AM.

If ever there was a time for a line to form, now would be it! What a grand location to even have a line. It could wrap around the peeling edges of mustard wallpaper and curve alongside the building, coming to a starving end right outside of the 2nd Avenue deli that I live above. What a deal–win my heart over and then we can go halves on a pastrami and rye sandwich.

The truth is, I'm sick of YOU complaining to ME that you're single and I'm even more sick of ME complaining to ME that I'm single. I'm equally sick of convincing myself that if I spend all my free time watching *Keeping Up With The Kardashians* that somehow, someway, I'll be putting myself out there in the universe and be attracting the attention of the male species.

The reason most of us are STILL single: Evaluate where you spend most of your time. Who you spend it with. What you do while you're there. If your answers include: alone, with my girl-friends, at crowded bars talking in a closed circle, or watching Netflix in between your couch cushions, then there's your answer.

There will come a day when you'll find yourself buried underneath empty ice cream cartons and self pity that you'll kick the wallowing bucket and allow yourself to realize if you want to change, if you want the boys to start knocking on your door, you have to find them, dazzle them, grab them by their sweaty thumbs and teach them how to knock. You have to, as my ballroom dancing teacher once tried to teach me how to do: grab a hold of a partner and mirror their lead.

A little over 8 months ago, I was twirling around the city thinking I had a grip on being single. Answering my friends, who would ask the same question as my mom, *since you're like perpetually, always, really single, have you thought about trying online dating?*

NO.

It was one of those quick no's that are rare exceptions to our usually indecisive minds. Kind of like when Time Warner asks you if you're okay with them transferring you to someone else, which will mean you'll have to be placed on hold, again, for 45 minutes.

No. No. No.

Okay, fine. I thought about it. But I wasn't convinced that I should set up a profile and write some witty jargon to try to sell myself to a pool of guys over the internet. It would be like creating an advertisement for a billboard in Times Square, except instead of a million tourists gawking at it, strange men would be. But, I was having a hard time meeting people the other way, partially because I spent too much time working and partially because I had grown hostile to meeting guys at bars who were three tequila shots in and slurring their words while petting my hair.

A month later, I had a profile up on JDate.

Online dating wouldn't be so bad if people just spoke to each other like humans. As if they were meeting in person for the first time. If I was at a bookstore and a guy wanted to approach me to say hello or get my attention, if he said something like, "Sup Cutie. You fine." And followed it up with a wink face, I'd be confused, embarrassed, and ultimately walk away. If he said something simple, something that's not forced or creepy, something as blasé as, "Hey, what book are you reading?" he'd get my attention and along with that, my response.

But instead, guys are sending messages like this one that I received:

I think it's only fair that I give you full disclosure…I'm an asshole 0=)

That's what this guy by the username The Goblin sent me as a first message, as if that even warrants a response. Was he thinking I'd reply back with a *PLEASE take me out. You sound like a lovely, respectable human being*?

Or this one that I received shortly after:

You're 5'6? too tall for me, sorry.

If you want to be a successful online dater, stop with these kinds of messages:

1. One World To Rule It All

Sample messages: *"Hey"; "Yo"; "Sup"*

They looked at your profile. Not really. They looked at your gallery of photos, liked what they saw, didn't have enough time, or energy, or a need to read anything about you so they just sent you one word.

2. I Hope Your Looks Don't Lie

Sample messages: *"Yo. You're hot. That really you in those pics? Hope you not Catfishin' me."; "If you can talk as good as you look, I may be in love."*

3. Misused Punctuation

Sample messages: *";)"; ":-@"*

When's the last time you actually winked at a real, live, girl? I hope the answer is never.

4. Copy-Paste

Sample message: *"Hey, Marissa. A little about me: I'm from Long Island and I used to play football. I like to go out with friends on weekends, but I also don't mind staying home and watching a good movie, with some good company. You look like someone I'd like to get to know better. Do you agree?"*

If you're lucky, like I always am, they will even forget to change the name on the message and you'll receive one written to a Marissa or a Francesca when your name is Jen.

5. Misery Looking For Company

Sample message: *"I'm not a fan of online dating, but I figure I'd give it a try"; "How's JDate working out for you? I don't want to do this but my mom paid for my account and pesters me every day about it to make sure she's getting her money's worth."*

6. What Did You Just Ask Me?

Sample messages: *"Other than your looks, what are three things you've got going for you?"; "If you were on Jeopardy, what would be your 30 second speech when Alex Trebek interviews you?"*

CHAPTER 12.

A WEEK WITH A 100% HONEST
ONLINE DATING PROFILE

"Do you want to know what your problem is, Jen?" She says to me over Gchat.

I don't even know her – *she doesn't even know me*. She's just a friend of a friend of a friend who occasionally reads the writing that's posted with my byline on the Internet.

It's 11:20 am on a Tuesday. I'm at work drawing snails on a tiny notepad trying to decide whether I want to eat a cinnamon bun the size of my kneecap or a slice of cheap pizza for lunch.

"Your online dating profile must look like a disaster," she types back to me within seconds of my question mark response. *"That's why you're not meeting anyone. That's why you are still single!"*

I've decided to make t-shirts that say "Team Jen: helping her find a boyfriend since 1988," since it seems that everyone, everywhere, has taken on my relationship status as their personal philanthropy.

57

It's as if something about me screams single and unable to properly mingle on my own. I have more people pitching in to help out with my single girl status than I do fingers on my right hand. There's my mom, my rabbi, and my best friend who recently got engaged. Even my cleaning lady asked to take a picture of me around with her to query the residents of other apartments she goes to.

Now this girl?

There's nothing wrong with my online dating profile. If anything it shines this Instagram-like filter over my life making it look flawless, exciting, everything but the mundane way I really spend most of my free time: stuffing down $1 slices of pizza and lounging around in my fleece pajamas watching season after season of *Mad Men* on Netflix. What does this girl want me to do? Use a picture of Heidi Klum in a bikini as my main photo and write an extremely vague description of my hobbies like everyone else does: *I love to go out – but I also love to stay in* (ugh, boring).

I've never been very good at listening to other people's advice — especially when it's unwarranted. If someone tells me to turn left instead of right, I'll turn right just to see what I'm missing out on. Just to see what it was they didn't want me to see, to feel, to experience.

So minutes after she tells me what she believes is my ultimate problem, I eat a giant cinnamon bun the size of my kneecap and decide to give my online dating profile a makeover. I decided that I'd write up a profile of what I would actually say about my interests and myself if I was being 100% completely honest. Here's what it looks like:

User Name: *MyMomMadeMeDoThis1234*

Age: *27 – but when I have a cold I can easily revert back to being 4-years-old or if I'm out at a bar and I hear "Don't Stop Believing," I can easily transform back to acting like a college freshman.*

Location: *Sitting behind my Mac Book Pro trying to scratch off the dried up smear of peanut butter that's made itself at home in between the G and H key.*

My Details:

My hair is: *Blonde. Okay, fine – it's really more a Jack and Coke color but every three months I march my butt to the salon and give some nice hairstylist a chunk of my paycheck to make it look more like champagne.*

Body type: *Fits very nicely on an L-shaped couch.*

Weight: *umm, before or after I just finish a medium pizza all to myself?*

In My Own Words

My Favorite Physical Activities: *I signed up for a gym about a year ago and pay them $40 of my hard* *earned money every single month – so technically part of me (my wallet) goes to the gym.*

I'm Really Good At:

- *Knowing all the lyrics to Jay-Z's Hard Knock Life album.*

- *Writing what I want to eat in Haiku format on napkins at fancy restaurants.*

- *Fumbling around in my purse trying to find my wallet when the bill comes on a first date.*

My Perfect First Date: *One that doesn't start with you name dropping your ex-girlfriend and end with your guacamole stained chapped lips suction cupping my ears because I turned my head when you went in for an unwarranted kiss.*

My Ideal Match

Drinking Habits: *Doesn't smell like stale tequila. Doesn't spend the majority of his Friday night hugging a toilet seat. Doesn't drink like a sorority girl on a "Neon or Nothing" social.*

Relationship Status: *umm 100% single. What kind of question is this?*

Job: *Has one.*

Hobbies: *Also has one (or a few).*

Must love*: Me – a girl who spends too much time on Twitter, owes an extraordinary amount of money in late fines to the library, only wants to ever eat pizza. And yourself. Please love yourself first.*

But before I pounced on the delete button and erased my old profile, I decided to do a weeklong experiment. I'd put up two profiles, on two different—yet comparable and similar—dating sites, and see what happens. One that was my real profile – with information about myself that doesn't make me sound like a lazy, pizza obsessed girl and one that has the same details from above and see what happens.

Here's the breakdown of the 7-day experiment.

One-Week Experiment	Real Profile	100% Honest Profile
Generic Messages	17	15
Profile References	6	21
Strange Messages (*pick up lines)	7	10
Total Messages	30	46

My real profile fielded the same old bland messages. If someone did break away from the "Hi, how are you?" or "You look cute" mold, they only mentioned something brief and nonchalant about something I wrote in my profile like how

I'm from Florida or love pizza (that's the only fact about me heavily stressed in both profiles).

With the 100% honest profile, the majority of the 21 people who mentioned something that I wrote, added a notable comment like:

"Gotta give it to you, you have by far the most entertaining profile I've seen on here. A good sense of humor is one of the sexiest things I find about a girl. I'd love to get to know more about you. Hope to hear from you soon." –JB-ROD

"I love how casually you talk about yourself. Truly shows how confident and free spirited you are. Best profile I have seen this far and you seem like a ball of fun to be around." –PJ71P

I still received my fair share of generic messages with the 100% honest profile –proving that some people don't make it past your photos before shooting you a message. And of course I got my fair share of strange messages. I even had a few from people who recognized me from the other dating site, and one person who even recognized me from the gym.

After a week of dissecting these messages and accepting the fact that a chunk of people in this great big world now know the *real* me before actually having met me, I realized it's better to be more honest. Or at least a bit more fun when writing about who you are.

When you meet someone in person, it's messy. You won't look like the five pictures you chose for your profile and your answers to their spur of the moment questions won't be rehearsed. You won't have the time to write out what you'd like to say and read it before rereading it before finally getting the guts to press the send button.

In person, interactions are raw. They are genuine and often they are a bit intimidating. That's how your profile should look, should sound, should feel.

Fine, go ahead; roll your eyes at me. Have your best friend proof read your "About Me" section to make sure you don't sound like a total freak and have your other best friend Photoshop the beauty marks off your photos. But then, ask yourself, what's the point?

I've been on several dates with people I've met online and within seconds of saying hello and giving them a hug, I could feel that they were disappointed. That they were hoping for the polished girl in the mini dress with a fresh face of makeup and a carefully edited personally. You know what happens on dates like this? They become so terribly awkward and uncomfortable that you go home and threaten to quit dating for the rest of your life. In the end, they are a gigantic waste of time.

At least this way, with a profile that's as honest as my 93-year-old Great Aunt, the guy on the other side of his computer knows what he is getting himself into. Knows that the girl he'll meet in person will be candid. Will be a bit unrevised.

The other thing I learned from this experiment was that there really is someone out there for everyone. That even with a brutally honest profile, there were still guys who were excited about asking me out and getting to know me better. That regardless of how I looked in my carefully chosen photos, that they found me to be something other than extraordinarily bizarre. They found me memorable and to some degree, a breath of fresh air. And this time, I really truly knew they were talking about *me.*

CHAPTER 13.

LOVE IS BLIND

They say love is blind but really who are we kidding?

Love is more like those spinning rides at carnivals that strap you down and swirl you around until you're blue in the face. Or that feeling you get after you stuff your mouth with too much ice cream and suddenly your cranium gets frozen. Or the nervous shakes your hands fall victim to, as you're about to move a block during the game Jenga. To be precise, love is exactly like acid reflux.

In a city that attracts millions where everyone is moving to the beat of an Avicii song, sometimes the only way to meet new people is to be forced to enlist in a matchmaking service. I signed up for Grouper, a company that arranges a blind date for you and two of your dearest friends with another lad and his two friends, uniting Sgt. Pepper's

Lonely Hearts club for a night on the town, hoping that each finds their respected math.

I felt confident and calm having my two good friends by my side when this group date started, snapping me back down to earth when the nervous jitters started to affect my personality and my sweat glands, as we waited for the three men of mystery to join us.

And that we did. We waited, and waited, and waited until 35 minutes past the meeting time, they decided to show up.

Three disgruntled guys in button-down shirts with shaggy hair and bloodshot eyes approached our table and without introduction, a standard 'my name is' or a friendly handshake, they plopped their butts down.

The spokesperson of the group, the one wearing a light pink shirt that was fully unbuttoned, exposed his tangled chest hair, looked me in the eyes, did a wavy wiggle on his chair and blurted out, *So girls, what's your story?* A rush of stale whiskey and a pinch of sour tequila hit my nose and I realized these guys were straight-up-on-the-rocks-drunk.

That was the only full, sensible question or statement any of the boys made during the date. Everything else came out slurred from their mouths and left off important parts of a sentence: nouns, verbs, and punctuation.

What do youuuuuu work? One of them spit out to my friend Michelle, who politely replied with a smile that she plans events for a local hospital.

So you're a nurse? And you save lives? I have a lot of problems that I think could use your help with, he managed to say.

We tried to play connect the squiggly dots and carry at least one full conversation with these boys before giving up. But one of them lost his cell phone and started to crawl around on the sticky floor, the other had one eye closed and the other flickering open as he began to sink deeply into a REM cycle, and the last boy, the one sitting directly across from me, was flooding his mouth with shots in between every other word.

I sat there motionless. What seemed like a good idea to pull my girls and I off the couch on a weeknight to flirt with the New York City dating scene, was turning out to be a gargantuan category 4 disaster. When the guy across from me started to burp the first half of Happy Birthday To You, I told them this night, this date, this whole thing was over.

I pulled the plug. Pressed the off button. Picked up my belongings and told these guys sayonara. This uncomfortable, awkward, not going anywhere but their heads resting on the porcelain edge of some bar's toilet kind of night, was officially coming to an end after a record 23 minutes.

67

Anyway, it was 9:30 pm on a Wednesday night and this was a gigantic waste. The ice cream shop closed at 11 and I wanted to finish my three-week overdue library book. These belligerent guys were now simply using up my time, my energy, my conversation skills and my liver.

I'm not swearing off dates. Whether they come via a hip matchmaking service, an online dating site, or the offline way of knocking over someone's coffee and having them ask you out—*that still happens, right?*

It's just that the most fantastic people that I've spent time doing cartwheels with in this world, I've simply just met along the way. On a cold night in a small warm spot in Minnesota, while eating a slice of vegetable pizza on the Santa Monica Pier, while painting a house with Habitat for Humanity one Saturday morning in college.

I ended this group blind date in the same fashion that I've learned to medicate all awkward situations, by digging my spoon into the very bottom of a cup of soft serve. And with every bite, I realized even more that there is truly only one rule when it comes to love—when it comes to where, and when, and how to meet someone and then, once you've found them, how to fully recognize how you deserve to be treated.

Open your eyes.

CHAPTER 14.

9 UNUSUAL WAYS TO DESCRIBE WHAT FALLING IN LOVE FEELS LIKE

1. When you're on a crowded subway at that too early hour in the morning and your face is submerged in someone else's armpit and your toes are being crushed by someone else's feet and all of a sudden, right in front of you, a seat opens up. And as you're sitting down, eye level at all the briefcase commotion, you feel as though the chaos can salsa around you and it wouldn't even matter. You'd feel safe. You'd feel detached. You'd feel exceptionally content.

2. Draping clothes that came straight out of the dryer on your overworked and exhausted body. The way something so familiar can make you feel so fresh and so renewed. Can rest so blasé on your curves and hug onto your shoulders and make you feel complete.

3. Getting packages in the mail from back home during summer camp. Pulling your sleeping bag over your head and slicing open a box filled with candy and lanyard and stuffed animals that'll keep you from going bonkers over bug bites, nasty camp food, and girls around you going through puberty.

4. The first couple of seconds on a rollercoaster as your cart climbs slowly up the lift hill. Leaning back as your pumping heart is making a scene and you're building up the strength to scream and you're wondering if you can't turn around now, if you can't press the stop button and slide back down, if you could at least stay in this spot for a little while longer.

5. When you really, really, have to pee but the line at the bar is 17 girls deep and your legs are crossed and you're doing a little jig that reminds you of the unforgettable dance moves the guys used to do at your Bat Mitzvah.

6. Taking a shower after a long day (at the beach, or at work, or from forcing yourself to do something that scares the heebie-jeebies out of you). How the warm water splashes your pores so delicately that you close your eyes and pretend you're somewhere else.

7. When your airplane arrives at your much anticipated destination and you're so excited that

your legs are starting to bounce impatiently and you're trying to squeeze between an arm rest and a carry on bag to get off the plane and into the arms of the person waiting for you at the other side of the airport.

8. Though falling in love, sometimes, can feel a bit like acid reflux. Your chest will begin to burn and it'll suddenly become quite difficult to swallow. And it'll be the most uncomfortable feeling—while it lasts.

9. But maybe it's also similar to that feeling when you wake up at 3am and realize you don't have to get up for work yet. That you still have time to go back to where you left off and try again. Fall gracefully into that dream you'll try hard to make sure your alarm clock doesn't allow you to forget.

CHAPTER 15.

STOP ASKING ME WHY I'M SINGLE

Dear Mom, friend who recently got engaged, cat-calling guy standing behind me at Chase bank, Rabbi who I recently saw at Yom Kippur services, among others:

Stop asking me why I'm still single.

As if being single is something to be so massively ashamed of that I might as well wear a t-shirt that says someone who loves me very much went to Paris and got me this shirt because I'm still single.

Or a crime.

Who would have thought? Not finding anyone worthy of sharing the other half of a love seat with you while you feed each other fried artichoke hearts and laugh like chipmunks over Modern Family is worthy of doing time in the state penitentiary?

You say it like there's something seriously wrong with me; something that's been accumulating for a while and I didn't work hard enough to prevent, like Athletes Foot. It's as if you're about to dazzle me with a gorgeous compliment, and then you take it back. Rip it right out of my hands like a molten hot chocolate chip cookie, fresh out of the oven, at 2 am. Here's what you sound like when you ask me that question:

Jennifer, I'm so proud of your promotion at work. But honey, why are you still single?

I'm so happy that I'm not single! But don't worry Jen, I'm sure you'll find someone. I was talking to [insert friend's fiancés name] and he totally could not fathom how you could STILL be single.

Girl, you're too pretty to be standing in line here, all by yourself. There's no way you're still single?

Jennifer, oy vey, I haven't seen you since your mouth was covered in braces and your face in pimples at age 13, how could a mensch like yourself still be single?

Maybe it's some kind of twisted SAT question: If $X=3$ and $Y=12$, solve why Jen is still single in the equation: $X + SingleJen = Y$

Are you looking for me to rattle off a list of all the things wrong with me or my actions on first dates? You know, I was feeling pretty fine and dandy about myself today, but since you asked, I'm probably still single because:

1. I'm too driven with my career and I spend more time smooching my computer than I do humans.

2. Maybe I'm too open on first dates with the things I say: like my stance on the current state of our country's economy and how I owe a ridiculous amount of money in late fines to the New York Public Library.

3. I guess I'm a bit clumsy. But not in an *aww, she's so cute, someone go get a mop and clean up her spilt glass of Pino* way. But in an *umm, I hope you didn't love that button-down J. Crew shirt you're wearing because I don't think steak sauce comes out easily, and I'm sorry?* way.

4. I don't like to play games, other than Battleship and Black Jack, so when I don't wait 5 hours before texting him back or pay for dinner on the second date, I can hear the self-help dating books screaming at me on the top of their lungs, but I just don't care.

Maybe you should start putting yourself out there more, you say, on repeat—as if you don't appreciate my couch plopping Saturday night specials, *go to some local single events or pick up a new hobby.*

So mom…engaged friend…creepy stranger on the subway…Rabbi Yehuda, listen up: just because I'm in my mid to upper 20's doesn't mean that I need to be 6 months away from slipping an engagement ring on my finger. It doesn't mean I need to have the job with the 401K, the boyfriend who calls me "babe," and the 2nd floor walkup apartment on the Upper East Side. It means one thing and one thing only: I still have a few more years to figure it all out.

So leave me alone.

Or don't.

But just stop asking me *why I'm still single.*

CHAPTER 16.

8 THINGS I WISH I TOLD YOU ON OUR DATE

---

1. I saw you pick your nose. Which really isn't a problem, necessarily. Except, you, my friend, were digging for some serious treasure up there. And then, you so kindly shared the wealth with me while we were partaking in eating cheesy nachos as our "foreplay" appetizer. So when you asked me why I wasn't so eager to go to town, to go chip for chip with you during our little share time, that's why. They say *you are what you eat* and I'm certainly not your gushy green booger. *Moving on.*

2. You lost me at "My ex-girlfriend." I'm all about name-dropping on a first date. *Romney. Ruther Bader Ginsburg. Ryan Reynolds (as my imaginary boyfriend).* But when you bring up *she who shall not be named* and tell me about your three week vacation to some sunny island like Antigua, and then pull up a photo collage of you and this girl in a bikini (who is, of course, 1/3 my body weight), and end this mangled tale with the concurrent knowledge that this took place only 17 days ago, I suddenly lost my appetite, again.

3. Well, that was awkward. You know, when you walked me home and right in front of my doorman building you went in for a smooch and I, well I turned my head. And so, the edges of your guacamole stained chapped lips suction cupped my ears. Yes, I did feel your moist tongue swipe my cochlea and because of that, I may never hear the same.

4. I already knew that about you. I Google searched you and then crosschecked my findings with the local police department. The world is filled with whack jobs and I'd like to do everything I can beforehand to ensure myself that I'm not spending the evening with a serial killer. And in doing so, I also picked up the knowledge that you were a varsity lacrosse champ, recently attended your sister Kristin's wedding in North Carolina, and enjoy mixing your Coca-Cola with 7UP. It's really creepy how much there is on the Internet about people. If this bothers you, you could at least consider deleting your MySpace account.

5. The apartment you walked me home to isn't mine. Please see above for further explanation.

6. My hair really isn't blonde. Your online dating profile says you prefer to date girls with champagne colored hair. Well, naturally, mine looks more like Jack and Coke.

7. Your dating profile also says you're 6'3. I guess we all lie, a little bit huh?

8. There are a few things I didn't tell you, about me. I don't eat meat. Red wine puts me to sleep. I'm still in love with my ex too. My lips tremble like a broken record when I'm nervous. I get violently uneasy on dates when the bill comes. *But I bet you noticed that, didn't you?*

CHAPTER 17.

WHY DATING EXIT INTERVIEWS SHOULD EXIST

The other day, while deep conditioning my hair in the shower, I began to think long and hard about what I did to mess up my last date with this guy I was starting to like.

We went out twice and after our second date, I dialed three people from my favorites list to tell them all about it.

That sounds crazy, doesn't it? But it's not. I go on dates, every so often, and after most of them, I want to toss my iPhone across the living room and tip toe into a time machine to go back three hours and pretend none of it ever happened. I'm left feeling discouraged, hiding between my couch cushions, digging a spoon deep into some Cherry Garcia.

But this guy was different, and after our two dates I found myself over the moon excited to see him once again.

But I didn't hear from him. So I texted him a few days later and he responded with only one word and then nothing at all ever again.

I got the hint. I totally and fully understood that he was not into me. But what happened?

During date two we were laughing so loudly that the waiter at the restaurant asked us to keep our voices down. We were making plans to take over the universe, starting with a future trip to explore the hidden rooms at The Museum of Natural History.

If I brought this problem to the brunch table for my girlfriends to dissect, they'd assure me I didn't do anything wrong. That I'm a perfect princess and clearly he wasn't ready to handle someone so awesome. Clarissa would say that clearly he's not over his ex. Shannon would say he's probably really busy with work. Michele would probably go with the line that he's some kind of alien and secretly lives on Mars and is not ready for a long distance relationship.

Now that last one sounds crazy, because it is. But that's what our friends are for, aren't they? They are the padding on the walls for us to slam into and then bounce off of and be just fine. I'm thankful for that.

But after this date, I wanted to know what I really did wrong. I thought about maybe emailing him and saying something like, "Listen — I get the hint. I mean I saw that you logged back on to Tinder three hours after our last date (OK, I'm done with the crazy). Clearly, I blew this and I'd appreciate it if you could tell me what I did wrong. So that in the future I don't do it again, or I'm aware when I'm doing it or I work on censoring it. Throw me a constructive criticism bone here, will you?"

I guess I'm not ready to do that — yet. So instead, while I was in the shower deep conditioning my hair and contemplating what I did to mess things up, I came up with this dating exit interview that I hope to have the courage to send to the next guy who gets my heart pumping, then leaves me cold.

Jen Glantz's Dating Exit Interview

Name   (*required):
_____

Length of time "dating" Jen Glantz:
_____

Reason for leaving (*Select at least one)

Lack of interest: She talked about three P's I couldn't care less about: poetry, pizza and punctuation.

Better opportunity: I'm not ready to kick my Tinder addiction. I even tried to swipe right at a girl I met, in person, last night at a bar.

Relocation: She says she's from Florida like it's some place special. Would I ever consider moving there? I don't know. Maybe when I'm 65 and my only handicap isn't on the golf course.

Better compensation (salary/benefits): She's a writer. I'm looking for a sugar momma or a stay-at-home momma. Not someone who has a work to-do list that resembles some people's Costco grocery list.

Lack of advancement: She didn't have any "game" and didn't lend me any flirtatious gestures. When I went in for a kiss, she turned her head and for two seconds, my tongue got real intimate with her cochlea.

Lack of training and development: If dating was a course in school and it was pass/fail, Jen would fail.

Working conditions: There might have been a stain on her silk gray blouse. There certainly was lipstick on her teeth for a good 45 minutes.

Job-related stress: Our debate over ObamaCare got so heated, the people at the table next to us asked to move to a quieter, less hostile location.

Other.

All of the above.

CHAPTER 18.

FROM AUDITIONING FOR 'THE BACHELOR'

...Are you still single?

It's 9:30am. On a Monday...

Excuse me?

...and I'm at work.

Jen, this is Malissa, are you still single?

Her raspy voice beating against the other end of the phone sounds distant; unfamiliar as it is unflattering.

You must be friends with my mom; I'm guessing part of her Tuesday Mahjong group?

This isn't the first time I've received a bizarre call like this. Last time, it was a friend of a friend of my moms who desperately wanted to set me up with her NJS–Nice Jewish Son–who lives on the Upper West Side and works in finance—*how original.*

Listen, tell my mom thanks for trying, really—bless her heart. And I'm sure your son is a real Mensch, and everything, but I'm not interested.

By now, it's my fault that I'm still surprised by these solicitation calls about my marital status. When I first moved to the city, I signed up for a speed dating event and minutes later, my credit card company called to say they shut down my account due to suspicious activity—which was just me…trying to…date.

What? She blurts out suddenly, unpleasantly surprised by my allegations and fumbling over my lengthy early-morning monologue. *I'm calling from The Bachelor. We received your application and would like to meet you in person.*

I wish I didn't know what she was talking about. Or that this was just one of my unemployed friends first coming home from a late night, Lower East Side bender, prank calling me as they hunted refuge from a giant cup of coffee.

But then I remember it being winter. Being so wickedly lonely; watching cotton balls of frozen water fall from the sky and becoming sick of only pressing my lips against ceramic cups filled with hot water and lemon.

I'm just doing this to help assess my dating strengths and weaknesses. I try to justify to my darling roommate as I fill out the 14 page application to be on the next season of *The Bachelor*. She doesn't seem fazed, as if living with me for a year has made her immune to these radically chaotic adventures that I insistently sign myself up for.

One of my coworkers is beginning to watch me watch the phone in sheer panic. I remember that I'm at work. I remember that Malissa is still on the other line.

Can you email me the information? I try to say unflappably, acting like this is a crazed call from my landlord about a crowd of mice roaming freely, again, in my ceiling. Something as dramatic, shocking, and absurd as the conversation Malissa and I are in the very middle of having.

6pm, Thursday, ABC Studios. She blurts out quickly, only giving me the pleasure of one breath. *Wear what you'd wear on a date.*

And Jen...

She says, as if we are longtime friends. As if we often browse the sale racks of Nordstroms together or regularly go halves on a Mandarin salad at the Cheesecake Factory.

...bring some charm with you, would ya?

***

My chances of getting on the show look slimmer than I am. Plus, I'm so stuck in my ways that it just wouldn't work. What I mean is that I enjoy eating carbs—which isn't to say that the girls that get on the show don't enjoy it, but they certainly don't look like they do. And the only shots I take these days are of wheatgrass, at Jamba Juice. Imagine this: Me. In a Forever 21 dress. Shoving down two slices of pizza and then, chasing it down with some grass right before a rose ceremony. I'd make the kind of TV that people can't take their eyes away from—but not in a good way—in a look at that break-dancing dog in the subway kind of way.

I call my manager—my mom, and tell her what's up. She's the one constantly telling me that when love knocks on your door, you have to give it a chance. And then, give it another chance. And then, well maybe just go out with him one more time.

So, here's love, ringing my cell phone, at 9am like I'm some kind of dial-a-date service. *Good enough, mom?*

So, love called. I tell her before I really tell her.

I just don't know about this. Which in itself is disturbing because in the 25 years that I've known my mother she has never not had an opinion about something. *You really would quit your job? You would want to deal with all that drama? You'd kiss all those guys?*

We're doing the tango with a game of 20 preposterous questions, until finally she ends it. She ends everything, most of the time, with: *Jennifer, remember to be classy, not trashy!*

***

My mom inspires me to make a list of things I refuse to do at the audition. It begins to read like a modern day version of the 10 commandments:
-Thou shall not lie
-Thou shall not smooch anyone
-Thou shall not take my clothes off
-Thou shall not cry—which seems like all anyone is ever doing on that show
-Thou shall let more than 5 girls give me a dirty look before I tell them something brilliantly ludicrous like, Honey, if you keep making expressions like that; your face will get stuck.

The morning of the audition I throw a dress in a plastic grocery bag and toss in a stick of lipstick. I slip the little folded list in my back pocket, I'm ready.

***

Everyone here is perfect in such a stunningly creepy way. In a way that after spending a few seconds scanning the room, makes you believe you're seeing the same person over and over again. Their white stained teeth, stiffly small grown up doll-like bodies, and adorably manicured hair, make them all look the same.

And then, there's me.

Fresh off the 1 train that I caught in Times Square during post-work rush hour. I can feel the remnants of someone else's sweat dangle down the front of my arm as coherently as I can feel my own sweat drip from the inner core of my armpit on the other side.

Most of your time spent at an audition is spent just waiting. Waiting for someone to call your name. Waiting for them to snap four photos of you and film you for five minutes.

So I'm spending time chipping away at my silver nail polish, making small talk with the most beautiful women alive.

Why are you here? I ask them in a non-accusatory way.

Dating is hard. One of them says while teasing the back half of her burgundy hair. And we all nod feverishly in agreement. *Maybe I'll find love on this show.*

And we all laugh uncontrollably at her. Until I notice, everyone is just me. I'm the only one laughing.

You don't seriously believe that, do you?

Everyone's silent. One girl gives me the eye-roll-hand-flip-whatever sigh and gets up to leave.

Note to self: I should have added at the top of my Bachelor commandments *thou shall try really, really, hard to not say exactly what I'm thinking out loud.*

I can tell I'm no longer wanted here. I excuse myself in search of comfort in which I quickly find, alone, at a table stacked sky high of free donuts.

***

The guy behind a pair of thick-rimmed glasses behind a flip camera asks me a couple of questions and I find myself rambling. In no particular order I mention: alligators, J.D Salinger, Croatia, Nicki Minaj, how fruity pebbles are amazing on top of mango ice cream. I stop. Only when he gives me the hand gesture of wrap it up, which is just a few steps above giving someone who is in the middle of speaking, the finger.

We're finished. Before he starts to disrobe me of the microphone attached to my pleather dress he pauses to say–

Jen...

As if we've done this before.

...you have lipstick on your teeth.

***

I leave the audition and barely make it three blocks east before my phone rings.

It's 9:30pm. On a Tuesday.

So, are you still single?

This time, the voice is familiar. Lined with a tone of warmth and worry; a tone only someone who loves you down to your stubborn core could string throughout a question like that.

Yes, mom. I am.

CHAPTER 19.

HOW TO DEAL WITH HEARTBREAK

Dear Jen,

I am going through a pretty ugly heartbreak, Jen. One thing I have learned is that taking advice from strangers is just as important as taking advice from friends because it reminds us we are not alone. For me, heartbreak feels like the most unnatural thing in the world. You create these intense and amazing memories with someone and even if you end on good terms there is still something so tragic about ending a romance.

The part where I become lost is what to do with all the left over memories and love?

Sincerely,

A.

Dear A.,

Every time I go back home to my parents' house in Florida, my mom always asks me to clean out my childhood room.

That room is quite the mecca of my pre-adult life. Push pinned into every wall, stuffed into every drawer, are artifacts from the parts of my life I've grown out of – or that have grown out of me. I'm talking love letters written in milky pen, tucked into yearbooks. Janet Jackson and Boyz II Men CDs and Minnie Mouse stuffed animals and clothes that wouldn't even fit my American Girl doll, let alone the bones of my 26-year-old self.

But every time she asks me to do this, I throw a tantrum.

"Why can't everything just stay like it is?" I say kicking and screaming. *"Why do I need to give things away and make this place look like the room of a grown up I'm not ready to be?"*

That stuff is all I have left. All of my deep-rooted memories live inside of the stuffed animals and polaroid pictures of people I haven't spoken to in years. That stuff, though most of the time I don't even remember I have most of it, gives me comfort. It reminds me, on occasion, of the parts of my life I've had to say goodbye to or have simply just expired and no longer make sense to say hello to.

That stuff is all I have left, right?

I'm not going to even begin to try to tell you how to heal heartbreak (as you can see, I have issues letting go) because I don't know how and I will stick my fruit-by-the-foot stained-tongue out at any of the people or books who try to preach those things to others.

Like you said, heartbreak is so terribly unnatural. Therefore, I imagine, there's no real cure or real trick to pull yourself out of it. I think the only way to get over it is to first simply sulk in it. Let it take over every single thought and bone and action of yours. Because even if you try not to and you do what your friends beg you to do: take a shower and put on pants, pick up a new hobby, or join them for a night of slamming tequila shots and grinding on the dance floor with a guy in a muscle tee, heartbreak – like acid reflux – comes out to play whenever the heck it wants to.

So give in.

I will tell you this – though at this moment, you won't want to believe me – it will get easier. It has to. Everything we go through at first seems so unbearably rough and disjointed.

Want to know why?

Eventually, we get used to things. We wake up one day and think, "OMG, I'm never going to be in love again or get out of bed again or be able to stop stuffing my face with these mighty fine Cheetos, and by week 47, you're going to find yourself on a 3rd date with a guy whose smile makes you realize your heart is still working quite alright and your sweat glands are still properly functioning and responding well to nerves.

But anyway, yesterday, I finally did it.

I cleaned out my room. I tossed things away that I never knew I could. Because I remembered, memories don't belong in things. They don't even belong in people. That's the coolest and most haunting part about them – is you don't actually need the person or place or thing to remember. You just will. You always will.

You two had darling memories together; I know that, because when you're in love, even the simplest and smallest thing can be the most delicate and strikingly gorgeous memory. You could be eating a ham sandwich that you got at Subway together on a park bench in the middle of August, as the leaves flirt with color changes, and never be able to forget it.

What I'm trying to say is you don't have to do anything with those memories—that love. They'll always be a part of you. Don't even bother trying to erase them *(spoiler alert: you can't)*.

We fall madly in love and we fall on the floor and madly cry. We laugh until we feel our world starting to spin and we do things that make our heart run a marathon race.

Don't do anything with those memories. And when you're somewhere, far away, and you see a muted green Jansport backpack that looks just like the one he used to carry around or you smell a hint of lavender and it reminds you of the time you got a massage together on a vacation in Denver, let yourself feel every part of it.

Let yourself remember.

Because memories are the closest reminder we have that we're alive.

We're so painfully and mesmerizingly and daringly alive.

All my love,
Jen Glantz

CHAPTER 20.

THE TRUTH ABOUT BEING SINGLE ON VALENTINE'S DAY

"Oh man, it looks like Valentine's Day is on a Friday this year," I say as we're going down, down, down. I'm riding the elevator with a platonic friend of mine, desperately trying to make conversation. I talk about how this is the sixth snowstorm to hit NYC this season before I mention that Derek Jeter is retiring before I finally mention Valentine's Day.

"Is it?" He says, so brilliantly blasé. As if he hasn't walked into a CVS in the past three months and been doused in the smell of packaged chocolate and the fur from all the cute little teddy bears didn't latch on to his black pants. "I really don't care much about that holiday, anyway."

"Yeah. No. Me either," I respond. Brushing off a topic that keeps me awake at night as the elevator door flings open and we both go our separate ways.

I've never been good at lying and I'm really, terribly, awful at lying to myself.

So, when all my friends (who are engaged) started asking me what I'm going to do on Valentine's Day this year, I fumbled to come up with something convincing. Something that wouldn't make them feel sorry for my sad, single self. Something that wouldn't require them to place their manicured nails on the small of my back and say, "Aw, don't worry, you'll have someone next year." Or, "Ugh, I remember when I was single on VDay — it was the worst!"

None of that, please. So, I told them: "Oh, you know. Well, I haven't really thought about it? Is it THIS Friday? Hmm. I'll probably just come home from work and watch *House of Cards* and eat a few cupcakes. Nothing too crazy."

Who am I kidding? I'll probably eat more than just a few cupcakes. I'll probably eat a third of my bodyweight in cupcakes and sprinkle on a few of those heart-shaped candies and any Hershey kisses I can get my claws on. And while I'm picking the sugar out of my teeth, I'll probably do something extraordinary like stalk an ex-boyfriend or cry over a montage of photos of my friends and I from college until there's icing all over my computer screen and the amount of high fructose corn syrup flowing through my veins is enough to put me in a sugar coma and I'll top the night off by laying in the fetal position beside my refrigerator.

Here's what really happens when you're single on Valentine's Day.

7 a.m.: You wake up. You toss. You turn. You check your phone and you see that you have no missed calls. No unread texts. Your phone buzzes. It's your dad. He sends you a text message that reads:
JEN, HONEY, IT'S DAD.
Happy Valentine's Day. I will always love you.
You gush with happiness. You start to believe this day won't be so, so bad so you decide to take a peek at Facebook. You see photos of people eating breakfast in bed. Of people with their guy in one arm and an overstuffed teddy bear in the other. You see one, no two, oh wait that makes three, photos of someone's brand new engagement ring. Ughh.

9 a.m.: You sit next to a couple on the subway while you're trying to get to work and they're trying to swap saliva. You actually hear the sound effects of their mouths suction-cupping each other. You actually swear a drop of their mixed up spit is somehow on your elbow. You make a face. You make your own sound effects. They don't pause for a second to even recognize that you exist. You feel the beats of their "No. I love you more" whispers pulsate in your eardrum. You want, no no no, you need a hug. There's a homeless guy with one shoe in the corner. Not him. There's a grandmother across from you. Hmm, maybe her. You see a guy in a suit with slicked-back hair holding a breakfast burrito. Yes, that would be nice. You decide to wrap your arms around your giant scarf instead.

Noon: You see the desks of all the other girls in your office sprout with fresh flowers like it's the first sign of spring. You watch them finger the delicate pedals of their roses. You contemplate touching the thorns. You listen to them say, "Here, Jen, take a few roses. I have a DOZEN more!"

"Well you know what?" You don't say. "I don't need your roses because I have a dozen donuts in the kitchen and I bought them for myself!"

4 p.m.: You hear the intimate details from the guy who sits across from you about how he has a reservation for two at some overpriced restaurant in the city where Jay-Z and Beyoncé went last Valentine's Day. You help him use Google Translate so that he can understand the menu and impress his date with what to order.

6 p.m.: You take a crowded subway cart back home and you're standing alongside a group of guys in their khaki work pants, clutching bouquets of beautiful flowers. A few of them are holding shopping bags from Victoria's Secret or Godiva Chocolate or Bath and Body Works. You wink at one of them because you want to declare how proud you are of him for making this day special for his girlfriend. He thinks you're creepy and walks to another subway car. You wink at another guy. He asks you if you have something stuck in your eye.

8 p.m.: You flirt with the delivery guy who rings your doorbell to drop off a stuffed-crust, medium-sized pizza. "Are you hungry?" You ask. "Do you want to come in for a slice?" He asks you to hurry up and sign the receipt. "It's Valentine's Day," he reminds you. "I want to get done with work so I can celebrate with my girlfriend."

8:15 p.m.: You're still hungry. You decide to order more food. Never mind. You decide to skip to dessert. You order a dozen cookies. You text a friend to see if they want to come over and eat half. They say they can't. They found someone for the night on Tinder. You text another friend. They say they can't. They are out taking shots with a bunch of frat guys at a local bar.

9 p.m.: You're in a sugar coma. You delete Instagram off your phone because you've seen too many couple-kissing selfies. Too many pictures of flowers. Too many hashtags that say

#myboyfriendisthebest   #hefinallyputaringonit
#ilovevalentinesday

9:45 p.m.: You start blasting music. You change the lyrics from "No woman, No Cry" to "No boyfriend, No Cry." You sing "Timber!" at the top of your lungs. Whitney Houston's "I Will Always Love You" comes on your Spotify playlist. You slow dance with stuffed animal moose.

10:30 p.m.: You decide to call it a night. You snuggle up into your bed. Your phone rings. It's your best friend from college. She just got engaged. "He put the ring in a soufflé!" She says. You ask her how the ring tasted. You close your eyes.

10:45 p.m.: You remember tomorrow is a new day. Chocolate goes on sale. People's roses will start to wither. All your friends will still be engaged and you'll still be single. But you won't care. It won't matter.

Until next Valentine's Day.

CHAPTER 21.

JEWISH "GUILT" FILTA FISH

I heard this charmingly chaotic love story once. Guy meets girl and guy really, really, relentlessly wants to ask the girl out. So, one afternoon he picks up the handle of his rotary phone, swings the dials until he hits all seven of her numbers and awaits connection.

Hello? She answers. As her only indication of who this person calling could be was the crackle of their voice traveling into her ear, the brief introduction they'd have to give.

He tells her his name before he really says: *I'm calling because I want to take you out.*

I'll only go out with you if, she says because when it comes to love you might as well make all of your demands up front. That way the person knows what they're getting themselves into right off the bat. *If you find someone to take my sister out.*

The guy wasn't expecting that. Not at all.

Your sister? He said with as much hesitation as frustration. But he was pretty determined to take her out, so the next afternoon he lined up a group of 17 guys from the neighborhood along the creases of the sidewalk and rang the girl's doorbell.

Your sister can have her pick.

***

The last thing my 94-year-old great aunt Rita ever said to me was:

Jennifer, as she pinched my cheeks and crammed a piece of freezer-burnt rugelach down my throat, *why don't you have a boyfriend? Huh! The boys must be lining up.*

Which were the exact same words that she started stuffing our conversations with ever since I turned 13 and was forced to read hieroglyphics out of the Torah to become a *legally Jewish* adult at my Bat Mitzvah.

Just a few weeks after she tells me that for the last time, I'm at her Shiva, standing in the dead center of a circle of Jewish women, who are acting like they just captured their evening prey. Begging me for my phone number to give to their very single, very good-looking, very Jewish sons.

Every Jewish holiday, gathering, or funeral, simply has two main goals:

1. To make sure you eat as much food as your expanding waistline can tolerate before becoming flushed with acid reflux, while still having enough leftovers to pack in a tupperware and store in your freezer for one desperately lonely night when you're brave enough to defrost the brisket or the matzo ball soup or the roast beef.

2. And second, and equally as important, to make sure—if you're single, and everyone will know if you're single—that you've given out of your phone number so that you can be set up with this person or that person, or, if you're extraordinarily unlucky, so that they can run your phone number and photo in the next newsletter for the temple.

The morning of her Shiva, I'm on the phone with my mom when she hears me interrupt our conversation to say, *oh my god, thank you,* to a nice pedestrian who picked up my scarf from the sidewalk.

What happened? Are you okay, Jennifer? She says frantically while I'm screaming over her panic in an attempt to let her know that everything is alright, which is what I'm always doing on the streets of NYC, as the constant sounds of sirens and honks are enough to rattle the peace of my precious mother who is living in Boca Raton.

I dropped my scarf and someone stopped to tell me, I fill her in.

Jennifer, was it a boy? Why didn't you stop to speak with him? You know, she says before I have the chance to tell her that no, it wasn't a boy, it was a little old lady, *you should really take your headphones out when you're walking on the street, you just never know who you'll meet when you're making a left turn.*

Right, I say before I think about some of the unforgettable people that I've met while walking on the streets.

A crazy guy on 57th and Lexington who screamed in my face and told me the world was about to end in approximately 11 minutes and the only way to survive was to dance around in circles.

A woman and a dog who were asking for money outside of Grand Central Station, who I stopped to chat with and ended up giving her $23 dollars and a Bed, Bath, Beyond coupon.

Oh, and a tourist who was walking in my direction in Herald Square and stuck out her hand to point at something and ended up clocking me in the face. We met, officially, when I stopped to let out a cry that my nose hurt and instead of her saying sorry, or anything, she shrugged her shoulders and kept on walking.

So really, the prospects of meeting my next boyfriend while running through the streets of NYC and avoiding broken bones is really unlikely.

But try telling that to my mother, who thinks every elevator ride, trip to the supermarket, workout class I go to is filled with eligible bachelors and I'm just being picky.

Our conversation ends with her telling me to wear something classy, not trashy or flashy tonight, because even though it's a Shiva, I never know who I'm going to meet.

And so, at my great aunt's Shiva, when the old yentas are lining up with napkins that they used to blot the lipstick and lox off their mouths and pens from the rock bottom of their purses, hoping to get my phone number to pass onto their Jewish sons, I don't budge with embarrassment or try to run away.

Look there's Jennifer, she just moved here and is single, one of them whispers loud enough that the Orthodox rabbi has to pause in the middle of a prayer to try to uncover the commotion.

Yes the blonde girl, another chimes in.

Maybe if you put down the cookies, my cousin tells me as she's parading me around in a circle, *you'll meet someone already.*

And I leave, but only after I've handed out my phone number to every lady there with a son.

How's that, I say to anyone who will listen, but especially to my great aunt, who I know must be here, somewhere. As I'm sure she's orchestrating this whole thing while eating clumps of freshly baked challah bread from her post up above.

Anyway, the girl's sister ended up picking a guy out of that lineup with copper colored eyes and a smile that would light up the core of her heart for many, many years. She picked him and just a few months later, she married him. As did the girl, who married the determined guy. The girl's sister, well she was my grandmother and the girl, my great aunt Rita.

ACKNOWLEDGEMENTS

Thank you to my first book agent who told me nobody would ever buy a book about messy dating stories. *All My Friends are Engaged* was an Amazon best-selling eBook for more weeks than I can count on my hands and my toes.

Thank you to my first writing teacher, who told me that I wasn't very good at writing and I should try something else instead. I stopped listening to you 500 blog posts and two books ago.

Thank you to the NY Public Library for letting me step foot in the door even though I am delinquent on my late fee payments.

*All proceeds from this book will go toward paying those fines – I promise.

*Any left over money will go toward funding my pizza eating addiction – so, thank YOU, in advance.

ABOUT THE AUTHOR

Jen Glantz is a 20-something writer living in NYC, searching for a guy who will look at her with the same kind of goo-goo eyes with which she looks at pizza. She's the heartbeat behind the website, The Things I Learned From, and the founder of the head-turning business, Bridesmaid for Hire.

You may have seen her before:
– Running down 5th avenue with a slice of pizza in each hand
– As the lead guitarist (alongside her adorable dad) in "The Jen Glantz Band"
– On JDate and/or Tinder
– Or on a giant poster hanging outside the New York Public Library, where she's wanted for an overwhelming amount of unpaid late fees

Say hello:
  jenglantz@gmail.com
www.thethingsilearnedfrom.com

Manufactured by Amazon.ca
Bolton, ON